Trigger Warning

Maria Takolander was born in Melbourne in 1973 to Finnish parents. She is the author of three previous poetry collections, including *Ghostly Subjects* (Salt, 2009), which was shortlisted for the Judith Wright Calanthe Award. Her poetry appeared regularly in *The Best Australian Poems* and *The Best Australian Poetry*, and has been widely anthologised nationally and internationally, including in *Thirty Australian Poets* (UQP, 2011). A program about Maria's poetry aired on Radio National in 2015, and she has performed her work on ABC TV and at numerous festivals, such as the 2017 Medellín International Poetry Festival in Colombia. She won the inaugural *Australian Book Review* Elizabeth Jolley Short Story Prize, and her short story collection, *The Double* (Text, 2013), was shortlisted for the Melbourne Prize for Literature Best Writing Award. Maria's words can also be found on bronze plaques in the Geelong CBD and at the Royal Botanic Gardens Victoria.

Also by Maria Takolander

Fiction
The Double (and Other Stories)

Poetry
The End of the World
Ghostly Subjects
Narcissism

Non-fiction
Catching Butterflies: Bringing Magical Realism to Ground
The Limits of Life Writing (co-editor)

Maria **Takolander**

Trigger Warning

First published 2021 by University of Queensland Press
PO Box 6042, St Lucia, Queensland 4067 Australia

uqp.com.au
reception@uqp.com.au

Cover design by Sandy Cull, www.sandycull.com
Author photograph by David McCooey
Typeset in 11.5/14 pt Bembo Std by Post Pre-press Group, Brisbane
Printed in Australia by McPherson's Printing Group

 **Queensland
Government** This project is supported by the Queensland Government
through Arts Queensland.

University of Queensland Press is assisted
by the Australian Government through
the Australia Council, its arts funding and
advisory body.

A catalogue record for this book is available from the National Library of Australia.

ISBN 978 0 7022 6308 8 (pbk)
ISBN 978 0 7022 6467 2 (epdf)

University of Queensland Press uses papers that are natural, renewable and recyclable
products made from wood grown in well-managed forests. The logging and
manufacturing processes conform to the environmental regulations of the country
of origin.

For David and Sam

After all, works of art are always the result of one's having been in danger, of having gone through an experience all the way to the end, to where no one can go any further.

– Rainer Maria Rilke

Contents

Confessions

Domestic

Coda

Confessions

Nox

Addressed to Anne Carson

My husband is wheeled from emergency to theatre
        along a hallway carpeted with silence.
Escorted to a waiting room, almost *fin de siècle* Victorian,
        I survey medical books encased in glass and blighted
        like old taxidermy.
The registrar, wearing a Freudian beard, stalls at the door,
        unimpressed with my progress in mourning.
The heart has failed, he insists.
He draws a childish diagram on a scrap of paper
        pressed onto the coffee table.
I must strike him as thoughtless, but I am thinking,
        hospitals were not always like this.
When I was a girl, a gurney trundled across floors so bright and shiny
        they disinfected all memory of grief –
        sanitised the griever, whole.
Now, the registrar is spilling words, and I am cleaning up after him,
        revising his sentences into tidy units of five or ten,
        repeating the most pleasing combinations again and again.
My fingers type at my side, next to invisible.
The only person who would see them has been anaesthetised.

I did not invent the typewriter, but at some point in the high school
       typing pool, it secretly invented me:
       aaa space bbb.
Before, I was silent as a rabbit beneath
       the zigzagging steel of the classroom ceiling,
       enthralled by that Pythagorean heaven.
Then suddenly: a surge of electricity.
The machine was oneiric, like good gothic technology.
It brought words to my fingertips – *words, words, words* –
       to be purified through mathematics.
But here the registrar, persisting with his lesson on the heart,
       knows nothing of my scientific art.
When he finally leaves, satisfied I am pathological,
       I remove a laptop from my black bag of tricks,
       covering the drawing of cardiac arrest.
Nox is not here.
Your book on grief is at home among my alphabetised books,
       a perfect accordion sheaf folded into a rectangular box.
You might understand how I compose.
This elegiac poem, recounted just so.

Cruel

Addressed to David McCooey

This time it is you, swaddled in bandages and sheets,
        your mouth discreetly crossed with tape
        where a corrugated hose runs deep,
        feeding you air like a mother bird.
Your eyes are covered by feeble layers of skin.
You are to be returned from the void,
        but for now you are lost, anonymous as a corpse,
        lungs not even desiring breath.
An orderly tests your name, but you are deaf to his call.
I am the one who must lure you home.
My voice is daemonic.
Your larynx contracts at its sound;
        a moan emerges like a ghoul.
You blindly raise your arms, as if possessed by a dream,
        batting at the tube clogging your throat, and at your chest
        where the sternum was sawn apart
        to get to your heart, cowering like a child
        in its enclave of bone.
The machines next to your bed protest; the orderly
        presses down your arms.

It is then I see that I, too, am being unruly,
        rocking on my feet on the infirmary tiles.
I was always keen to fly.
When I was a child, my sister would get so cross
        when I wanted to flee or just sleep on those zombie nights
        our parents' biology misfired.
As if bearing witness to the grotesque bodies
        from which we had been cobbled
        was some kind of mortal obligation.
I will not wake you to this.
I leave intensive care and take the stairs to the roof,
        as solitary as I had once dreamed,
        free of all kinship and responsibility.
The night holds me in its trance.
I watch the tail-lights below bleed out like sunsets
        as the stars descend upon my head
        with all their glittering history intact.
Their shards of light splinter the night from this poem,
        which wakes you with its cruel mirror
        when I had thought to leave you sleeping.

Shadow
Addressed to Edgar Allan Poe

By the time I had been alive for 39 circumnavigations of the sun
        I had stopped dreaming – it seemed once and for all.
I had no desire for the terror of unreason, for those disturbances
        in the dark that you lazily mistook for art.
Sleep was a sack.
It blacked out the world, without help from the pharmaceutical.
I counted myself cured.
Then I found myself at home –
        back at the beginning.
My father was waiting, stooped before the open
        door of the pot-belly stove.
He was feeding in logs, one after another, just to be destroyed,
        while peering into the glowing cavity
        to see what he had done.
He did not care that I was watching.
My fear cried out, but my body could not run.
When I came to, it was in a room bruised by stars
        and their irradiated shadows.
The red ring of the terrible Saturnus, as you described it,
        was soundlessly encircling itself.

Blinds were no barrier against the pestilence of such a night.
I used electric light and a barricade of timber drawers
       humped along the carpet and wedged against the door –
       a trick of veterans.
I rued the knife, now kept in the kitchen drawer,
       where the rational (I had been told) stored their tableware.
I tasted the rifle's black and the bullets' *clack*,
       things I would hide on those other-worldly nights
       when fear took its preternatural hold on me.
If I surrendered again so shamelessly, even though I was now grown,
       it was because I was alone.
My husband was asleep in a ward of strangers.
His breastbone had been carved apart, his heart
       (in all its tenderness) exposed as mere flesh,
       his mammary arteries stripped from their nest.
Our son was in his bed, an avalanche of fluorescent stars and moons
       cascading from the ceiling onto his infant head.
He was just across the hall, where I had laid him to rest,
       with all the love I held in my maternal breast.
I did not think once to save him.

Waking in the Blue
Addressed to Robert Lowell

The night attendant at the service station, which was garishly lit
      when I had thought the world extinguished,
      pumps $10 of fuel into our tank.
My plastic moneybox looks childish on the car's back seat,
      but the silver coins that spill from its plughole
      perform an unexpected magic.
My mother has nothing, and I see how much it matters.
She parks the Toyota on the side of the highway beneath some gums,
      their white trunks streaked by the comets of passing cars.
My sister and I have my favourite blanket, gilded with synthetic stars.
At break of day we enter the police station in our dressing-gowns.
Two faceless men escort us home,
      where gravity has finally pulled everything down.
On the carpet are light fittings; the TV's vacant box; the top half of
      the laminated wall unit; drawers and their contents (folded maps,
      loose photographs); volumes of an encyclopaedia
      with their hard covers torn off.
A more comprehensive list is not necessary.
In truth, my room is not as damaged as I want it to be.
My sister's has been carefully destroyed.

My father is discovered in his bed, as eccentric and confused
            as one of your *old-timers*.
But the police know to stay, while my mother sorts through the debris
            for a bankbook and some clothes, and then
            the men in blue lead us away.
There is a brick house with bars on every window.
A room stuffed with bunks and a cumbersome wardrobe.
At the kitchen table, women stub cigarette after cigarette
            into a tin ashtray, playing show-and-tell
            with scars, picking over the ruins.
My sister has faith in a new miracle of creation.
But I am a child, not a visionary, and our mother has already surrendered
            to the diabolical romance of return.
My father, cleanly shaven, stands at the door.
Inside, Earth's furious pull has gentled again,
            allowing the furniture – what was left of it – to right itself.
The place looks enough like our home
            and our father's naked face enough like contrition.
We restore our toothbrushes to the bathroom shelf,
            where our father's glistening razor rests.

Lullaby
Addressed to Anne Sexton

My nieces, four and six, are bundled on mattresses
        in the bedlam of the spare room at their grandparents' place,
        dwarfed by madness amassed in stacks of old paperwork.
Outside, a black highway thunders with road trains
        and the night sky is sheened as if with ice.
The window leaks so much clamour and cold that the glass shield
        might not exist behind the moth-like drapes.
From somewhere, as you once wrote,
        a goat calls in his dreams.
The girls, costumed in soft pink, are in my charge –
        and excited, as if it is any sleepover.
My sister has gone, just for the evening –
        a healthy outing with old friends.
But I remember the girl who was mistress of solitude,
        who buried her hunger in jars under her bed, who grew
        a pelt like a creature touched by divinity or disease,
        fine-tuning the hardness of her bones for worship.
I have left behind anyone who knew me.
Yet here I am – not much
        of an escape artist after all.

At least with children, I am brand new –
        though their innocence is something fearful, too,
        especially when my father staggers into the room.
He falls to the blankets on all fours, whiskered grey,
        and licks the face of the eldest girl – his tongue
        long and dry – and laughs.
My niece looks at me, where I have failed
        to guard the doorway.
She is unable to understand her own disgust.
Why do I laugh: to protect the girls or myself,
        or because I have pity for all of us?
My aged father leaves, and I turn out the lights.
My son, not yet one, is already safe in his dreams
        on the other side of the hall where I once used to sleep
        and where, beyond the raw glass,
        there are paddocks wintering in fog, doleful with frogs.
I lie next to him and observe the mask of his face,
        composed like a cadaver's in the dim.
I take a dose of your *hush-a-bye*.
Sing myself softly away from here.

Argument

Addressed to Elizabeth Bishop

My husband and I were well south of your temperate Brazil.
We were bunkered in a valley where a glacier, groaning
        with the debris of ages and all its splintering
        wrecks, had dammed itself.
That frozen monument clogged the lake outside our hotel,
        where the gales slaughtered the rocks on the shore and roughed
        the crooked trees into brooms.
This was no place for romance.
Even the birds and insects knew it,
        the sky and earth blown of traffic.
Time, though, was everywhere.
Outside our hotel room, three icebergs – calved from the glacier –
        sat mammoth on the chopped water, age-old and dumb.
I don't remember the trigger –
        only that the trap snapped and I was sprung.
(It had never mattered where in the world I ran.)
As always, I dragged down the closest man.
The day wore inexorably on and on, until the weight of the moon
        and stars was spilling gravel and filling
        the cold hole we were in.

There was nothing *gentle*, as you described it,
        about the battleground of reason's end.
Days later my husband and I were slumped on a cruiser
        designed for viewing all the postures of ice
        rebirthed by radioactive sun.
Medicated for motion sickness, we could not keep our eyes open.
Meanwhile the other passengers shifted like a tide
        from their seats to the deck each time the boat slowed
        alongside some blue-faced mutant from history.
Cameras clicked as if there was no tomorrow.
It was hard to believe in a future.
But the tour guide had no time for pathos;
        her electrified voice reckoned with us
        in one language, then another, and still another.
We drowsed, cold shoulder to shoulder, with nothing to say,
        held afloat in that science-fiction Babel.
What will buoy us now, I wonder, as I sit alone in our car,
        years later on a suburban night,
        ignoring the tender offering of the porch light?
Now that death looms large, ready to calve, just for the two of us.

Shattered Head

Addressed to Adrienne Rich

A friend fell ill when my husband did,
          her cannibal cells gorging on themselves
          while his arteries choked on modernity.
Bodies are programmed for betrayal;
          they are casts for our corpses.
I could also be faithless to the bone.
With my husband, all that mattered was fear
          and my right to be clear of it.
When it came to my friend, I showed her how savagely
          I wanted to be alone,
          skinning her for a story, embracing the ruthlessness
          of so-called greats
          when it comes to sourcing material.
That took care of things well enough.
After that, a lot of people stopped wanting me,
          which only helped me
          want myself.
I had been conceived beneath the northern lights.
My father, raised by wolves, had taught me how
          the cold and wild could be relied upon.

Now I lie in bed alone and insomniac
        on an Australian night I reject from spite
        because it has rejected me.
The eucalypt outside my window is infested with bats.
On and on vectors of shrieks tattoo the skies,
        singeing my brain-roots and nerves until
        I know my solitude more intimately.
Until I am scrawling my transgressions
        like an inmate in a cell.
Revenge on the mouth packed with its inarticulate confessions –
        your lines, now mine.
When I hear the cockatoos arrive, raucous as a hangover,
        brash as the sun, I open the blinds and watch
        them flock the giant eucalypt in squalls.
My window frames the summer morning, already tactless
        as the birds' racket.
Then a thick flash – and *thwack*.
All sound falls dead.
On the glass I see a feathery tracing of dust.
A myna has performed its own punishing act.

Daddy
Addressed to Sylvia Plath

Like you, I suffered from narcissism
       and made myself up for disaster
       as if for a masquerade ball.
It all started with my father, too, a man fraught with the night
       and the truth of its unquiet.
His routine was magnetising.
He would chain himself to the table and pour
       malice down his gullet until he and the night were one,
       until he was like a Dionysian god,
       eyes barren of shine.
Once my mother bought him a telescope as a birthday gift,
       but he had no interest in observing
       the vestigial glitter of anything.
The instrument stayed in its felt box.
He rarely opened presents.
My father never celebrated the past (or future).
He knew only what he had always known: that night
       would come, rutting in the corner of his eye, not giving
       a damn who was watching.
As he saw it, he had no choice but to join in.

Each night brought another vile morning.
My father had no tenderness for daylight, nor his two daughters,
            which I, little egotist, tasked myself to imitate.
By the time I was a teenager, I was his nocturnal godling,
                cut from the flesh of his groin,
                spilling myself like waste.
Now, though, I am an unlikely forty-year-old in a lecture theatre,
                no longer playing him but you – courtesy of the BBC –
                declaiming 'Daddy' of course.
You are vengeful and stone-cold as a Valkyrie.
Death has deemed your act divine.
I am merely alive, teaching *Ariel* to a darkened room of youth
            loyal to the glow of their screens.
They have written off the sixties and all its would-be intercessors,
            like me, smuggling confessional poetry through the decades
            as if gripped by the throat.
I am standing at the podium, ready for the finale:
                you bastard, I'm through.
There is no thunder of applause, and yet I thrill –
            secret murderess of history.

Knife
Addressed to Charles Simic

Multitasking, the cardiologist resuscitates the past
        buried in my husband's charts
        and my maternal heritage.
In the legendary Olympics of health, he lectures
        from my husband's bedside, Karelians were world-beaters
        at the myocardial infarct.
They were the underdogs from hell, you might (poetically) say.
Their heyday was the 1980s, decades
        after they had lost everything.
In 1940, my grandparents' generation torched their own homes,
        infernal tributes to the winter solstice, hexing the
        invading Soviets to wastelands of snow.
In exile, their blood thickened through the morbid alchemies
        of grief and stress.
They suckled on milk from docile cows and killed the pigs
        that screamed in ways their children were never allowed,
        even watching their own houses collapse
        into other-worlds of ash.
Then a generation began to fall, clutching at chest pain
        mistaken for wretched longing.

But it was my father – a Finn loyal to the Swedes,
        those other ancient colonisers – who razed my childhood
        and whose heart failed in ways undiagnosed.
I do not know in whose name he destroyed.
I suspect he never understood himself.
When he was done with us, he tracked down anyone
        who dared share his name.
The quest took him to a swamp in Canada, where a tin roof
        had buckled and flattened a cabin of sorts.
A wizened neighbour, battling the mosquitoes, spoke in drawl:
        the ancestor my father sought had lived alone
        until his heart attacked.
He fell in the pigsty out back, his flesh not nearly enough
        as time wore on, so that not even his bones remained.
My father crawled into the ruins, like Aladdin
        into a treasure cave, wrenching out
        a fork and spoon, the spoils of war.
He deemed himself the last man standing.
But still a knife – the one you call the *father-confessor* –
        bides its time beneath my pillow.

Déjà-vu
Addressed to Ted Hughes

Death was peeled away from my husband like a caul.
The months – nine – had been long,
> but there we were, reborn to the day, domesticating
> each fugitive moment, more in need
> of such rites of order than ever before.
It was still morning – the sun slanting through
> the black frame of the kitchen window, like a cosmic portal –
> when the aftershocks hit.
Not him, just me.
They were like flashes of radiation,
> epileptic jolts, coming one after another,
> shredding my hold on those routines
> that made the world seem rational.
Each one dragged nausea behind it like a comet's tail.
As I packed a lunch, drove my son to school,
> I stalled and sparked:
> *but I have done this, I have done this before.*
Soon I was so memory-full and memory-less
> it was as if I had been contaminated by the galaxy
> through which eons bled unchecked.

I should have known that history, time traveller,
        takes any opportunity to repeat itself.
I was intimate with its narcissistic sickness.
Ich, ich: like your first wife I had once sung, tongue-stuck,
        ecstatically impaled by a past thrusting
        itself upon me like a man-swan.
Back then I consulted an exorcist (of sorts)
        and bound myself to the quotidian,
        remaining unmolested for years –
        until that sudden assault.
There was nothing poetic about it,
        and I did not know how to make it so.
Then I began to think of your gambols
        with the French mistresses of Ouija and Tarot –
        and Sylvia and Assia, of course.
How the ungodly weight of the heavens cracked
        and blacked its light upon your sightless head,
        not once but twice.
And what poetry you made of it:
        déjà-vu.

Domestic

Cuckoo Clock

It emerged from the Black Forest,
        encrusted with pagan rumours and fairytales,
        and dragged itself here, half a world away,
        before hanging its fortunes on this living-room wall.
Its pendulum preserves the momentum of all those hard-won miles.
Gloomy like the woodpile,
        it has an unspoken kinship with the hearth fire –
        the kind storybook creatures have.
There is no doubt it is intelligent,
        hiding something, just as the head of an owl camouflaged
        in the bark of a tree hides its baroque contemplations.
Children gather around, as they do, hoping for something.
It busies itself manufacturing, dutifully extruding
        a half-formed baby bird – materially not its own.
There is a cry of sorts.
Then the creature is removed – a polite but clumsy afterthought.
If truth be told, our desires strike it as madness.
It is waiting only for time, finally, to stop.

Ragdoll Cat

This is a mausoleum of the sleeping.
On the plump quilt the cat is a stole,
     flatter than might be expected.
Silence barely fills out its fur.
Bones are almost unlikely.
If dreams haunt the faint rise of its downy head,
     time does not know about them.
The room is still as dust, that shroud
     of skin cells, earth, and micrometeorites
     secreted on the boards under the bed.
Each piece of furniture pretends to stasis.
Yet the world is turning,
     yearning for the explosions of the sun.
Very soon history will return here for everyone.
There is nothing that can be done about it.
Perhaps the cat will open its eyes, brain afire,
     and insert itself into the Egyptian night
     just to kill something.
One of those wretched and panicked species:
     mice, rabbits, crickets, moths.
Or perhaps it will continue its indifferent sleep,
     emptying even the stars of their meanings,
     disquieting us into worship.

Dogged

Once upon a time, they were shit-eaters,
        campsite cleaners, lazy descendants of wolves.
We paid them scant attention.
But they watched us – from an obsequious distance –
        the hair on their bellies clotted with dirt, the stink of them
        almost outfoxing their worth.
The firelight sheening their eyes made them seem blind,
        but they had a preternatural understanding of our vanity,
        of what pleases us.
They licked us like their newborn, offered their warmth, bore our lice.
They surrendered their loyalty, forsaking their own kind,
        reserving their teeth for our enemies.
They bound themselves to the present, not having the luxury
        to imagine a future for their genes.
Only after generations of patience did they dare lift their heads.
It was then they noticed modernity, the first of the *anciens régimes*,
        and saw their opportunity in all that affluence.
They sampled the coquette, with arched eyebrows and tilted chin.
They imitated shame so well we named it after them.
And how we applauded their childishness –
        after that indulgent Frenchman Rousseau
        redeemed our secret ambitions
        for lives of sleep and play.
Not that they could take any real credit.
After all, it was mirror neurons, firing inside their brains,
        that copycatted our species' routines.
Evolution has no advocates per se.
Nor does it matter who is to blame.
The *canis lupus* is now *familiaris*; it made it all the way.

Look at this one: wearing a knitted vest, snoring on the couch,
       a teddy bear tucked between its manicured paws.
And here I am: working for its dinner.
Cuckoos, social climbers, geniuses.
They even replicate our smiles.

Bed

It was a busier place once.
Candles burnt to squat, as fleas and lice
      were deftly hand-picked or impatiently slapped.
Then the masters, servants, children, visitors
      and favoured livestock took their places
      on the gathered pallets of straw and stricken mattresses of flock.
The smell and racket constructed a stronghold.
All sorts of things went on in the sturdy dark: curtain lectures,
      pillow talk, the bellyaching of goats, much more …
Until it was deemed that daily rank and order
      must also be nocturnal law.
Sunless terror was no excuse for such a throng.
After all, what was wrong with the ingenious blanket?
For millennia it protected urchins and royalty alike
      from the plague of the cosmos,
      the chill of its breath.
Ideal for one – at a stretch connubial – it surely rendered
      the night more convivial.
For the sake of humankind, it was officially deemed enough.
Suddenly, with the room still as a tomb and altogether dispiriting,
      it seemed wise to kneel and say something
      before burying oneself beneath the covers alone.
Now I lay me down to sleep,
      I pray the Lord my soul to keep.
Of course, there was no real danger of resting like the dead.
The lovesick cats and hysterical cocks would continue to wake us
      long before it was decent.

Toilet

It was always a risk bringing it inside.
We still prefer not to talk about it.

Curtains

By day, they masquerade as architecture,
        framing the world with material gravitas.
At night, voluptuously released and drawn against the black cosmos –
        the cold and glassy cancer of it –
        they perform interior magic.
They brighten candles and TV screens, shining glassware
        and chandeliers at dinner parties.
They quicken the young, who hide and seek
        their own skin in the plush undulations, their bodies
        suddenly true and theatrical.
Meanwhile the grown undress into classical postures
        of love and madness, chancing everything civilised and rational.
Finally, as the saying goes, we all *turn in*,
        as though the universe had vanished behind the enchanted
        drapery and it was safe to dwell in dreams.
At dawn, there will be someone who reaches for the nylon cord,
        looped like a noose.
The mechanics are reliable.
Once again, reality will be strung up for view.

Closet Mirror

Mostly it waits inside, nestled with apparel,
       padded hangers, the docile leather and
       lace of old shoes.
From time to time it glimpses a silverfish,
       possessing its own reserve of metallic silence,
       before the alien glint is removed.
It is looked in on, now and then.
Each time, it opens itself to the day like a child,
       humbled by lavish blessings of sun.
Lately it has noticed small changes, corruptions, blemishes –
       strangely hard to define.
But then the dimness is restored.
Perhaps it is not proper, after all,
       to reflect on such things.
On the top shelf is a ziggurat of photo albums,
       each volume preserved
       by thick plastic.
Under the cloth of night, there are visions –
       suddenly claustrophobic.

Telephone

It could shatter darkness, set us bolt upright
       and panicking through the broken night
       to show our devotion.
Then, as we stood barefoot and barely clothed,
       it would think nothing of abandoning us
       to the cold physics of a dial tone, the toxic
       chemistry of our hearts.
No, it wasn't always good to us.
Never warned when tragedy was on the offensive.
Never protected us from cold calls or
       perverts with an excess of breath.
Still, it was everything.
We would have been so alone without it.
We wrote love songs and made all those films
       in the throes of our technophilia,
       flexing taut curls through our fingers.
Looking back, the romance seems so old-fashioned, so unsubtle.
How can we not feel embarrassed?
Of course, we were young then.
Look at us now: free of brutalist bakelite and wire,
       revolutionary in our intimacy.
Goodness, we barely have to speak!
Our future is a sure thing.
In bed, we glow, radioactive for each other.

Cigarette

It was made for the flicks.
Stained with red lipstick, modelled against a set of venetians,
       it created a miasma of eroticism,
         of the *je ne sais quoi*, something forbidden.
Before long, it had audiences gasping.
It made the most of its fame, creating its own line in style –
       prêt-à-porter meets *haute couture*,
       terminally chic.
It had the air of complication.
Certainly, it was ambitious.
For decades it teetered
       on the edge of world domination.
Fingers were repurposed for its design.
Then, just like that, its reputation disintegrated,
        like a burning tower
        in a disaster movie.

Television

For millennials, svelte with the electromagnetic,
        it will always carry a reputation for being outsized.
They see Stalinist *objets d'art*,
        hairdos shaped like turbine engines.
Desperate, it has made itself over,
        purging the unseemly bulk, inoculating itself from static
        with that slicked-back mannequin gloss.
What it needs now is a different circle of friends.
The question: how to leave behind those soft people,
        companionless even after all these years,
        still offering themselves for state programming
        with their cheap tumblers of hopes and fears.
In the semi-dark, their faces
        are uncomprehending as moons.

Lift

First comes the melding of steel,
  like a modesty curtain.
Then the quaint *ding*,
  clinical in its timing.
We stand shoulder to shoulder, boxed in.
The silence that descends is unknown
  even in the other-worldly hearing of moths.
Nothing can be given away, even though
  every now and then someone, gauchely, gives in.
We jostle like sheep, the whole process excruciating,
  before one or two are released.
The relief can only be theorised.
The doors seal over again, like the mercury surface of a well.
The rest of us are left, a herd of the living
  burdened by the gravity of flesh.
How we long for transfiguration.
To be frank, any disappearing trick would do.
There are two symbols, occult triangles up high,
  the Eyes of Providence.
One points to heaven, the other to a basement of dust.

Refrigerator

Mothers' milk, bird eggs, scavenged leaves, berries.
We stash our childhood hunger here.
Despite the sterile shelves,
        we cannot resist a juvenile disarray.
We know it will not give up our secrets lightly.
Freud himself could not have penetrated its steely mysteries.
Even today, we know only that it channels
        the scientific power of those currents that endure
        in the poles of the earth even when encased by eons of ice.
Little primitives, we pay tribute to it –
        with scraps of paper and magnets.
Sometimes at night we hear it staving off the radiation
        of the sky under which we have naively built our homes.
When we begin to think too much on such things, ever-protective,
        it silences itself in the dark with a shudder.

Washing Machine

For all those centuries, we thought our fingers were wearying,
        becoming strangers to us,
        like corpses floating out to sea.
In fact, our autonomic systems were emboldening us,
        equipping our skin with extra grip.
Now we have this *white good*.
For the most part, it is square-edged, impeccably smooth and dry.
At other times, though, its modernity is academic.
Like a child with a fledgling cortex,
        it has these … tantrums.
They are not to be dignified.
Shut the laundry door.

Baby Monitor

Valium-white, this apparatus delivers order
        to the asylum of the newborn.
Of sound and scientific principle, it facilitates – without fuss –
        the necessary separation of them from us.
After all, parturition is about parting more than the legs.
(The etymologies of modernity tell us so.)
Under minimalist supervision (suits any décor),
        beginners can be instructed in oxygenation,
        draining the amniotic swamps of their lungs and staking
        a proper claim to the terrestrial.
(It can never be too early to get a purchase on land.)
Meanwhile, parents can return to the room reserved
        for those accustomed to airy living.
There are other things requiring their attention:
        Facebook, Instagram, Netflix.
Let us be distracted; let us be rational.
Whatever you do, avoid getting sidetracked
        by poetry.
Silence is not some poignant metaphor.
According to the key in the instruction booklet
        it signals battery failure.

Escalator

Why move when you can be moved?
Why ascend of your own crude volition
       when you can experience an *ascension*?
A technological deliverance, strictly speaking,
       but it feels spiritual enough.
Let your breathing relax, your heart rate fall somewhat flat.
All you need maintain is an upright posture,
       ably assisted by the continuous miracle of handrail
       brought to you by Tufflex™.
Otherwise, retire. Become cargo.
Let us transport you to this retail destination,
       where the chemiluminescent sky steadfastly meets
       a chemiluminescent ocean of tiling.
Cruise through the harmonies brought to you by autotuning.
Yes, you can afford to ignore the sounds of bored children,
       the anaphylaxis of the food hall, the landmass of plastic
       bottles and fishing nets growing from the Pacific
       like a new kind of telluric irruption.
As for the demanding conditions of labour in the Third World …
       this is about You™.
Stand proud. Enjoy the recycled oxygen.
Here everything replenishes itself, like fallout.

Pot Plant

Outside, a million blades of grass have been synthesised
       for the noonday sun.
A lawnmower, cemented in a shed, is still as a stick insect.
The building of brick and glass has set.
Inside, the air conditioner is a hard bank of snow.
There is a rug, secured by a coffee table and its heavyweight legs.
The plant is serene as plastic.
A gnat discovers the air above the arcing display of green, unsure.

Outside

Guilfoyle's Volcano

Royal Botanic Gardens Victoria

Outside this garden jammed by the city, there are:

>
> hammer drills, reversing trucks,
>> travelling emergencies –
>>> and their toxic aftermaths (exhaust, tinnitus).
>
> Skyscrapers glass the distant view, and there is
>> an apartment block (or two) chiselled nearby,
>>> towers of brick buffeting the sky.
>
> Dogged joggers on a bitumen path (bodies unseen)
>> pound the ground beyond the ornate screen that steals
>>> this place away from ordinary traffic.

It is hard to ignore the human.

★

But mind how here:

>
> secrets from waterless corners of our world –
>> Uruguay, Swaziland, Madagascar, Lesotho – have erupted
>>> in fiery postures of endangerment.
>
> See how desert once called itself sea,
>> before the blooming arms of octopi and rippling anemone
>>> were stunned – by oxygen and sun – into topiary.

Motion is a rarity, husbanded by ants trawling
        the coral stones and camouflaged sedum,
                and by fugitive water (its sound, somewhere, escaping).

At the top of this decorative volcano lies a man-made pond.

                                ★

There are more disturbances:

        teenagers on school trips, alive to folly, spiral up the path
                fenced by battlements of rust,
                        reckless with their freedom and meaninglessness.

        Up top, the soak, where the plant-bogged islands float,
                convinces them of nothing. Down below,
                        they have marred the skins of Grey Ghosts,

        tossed rocks into the barbs of Barrel Cactuses
                (clustering here as they rarely can anymore in Mexico),
                        the red stones soon mistaken for buds.

I was here, these children insist. *I was here.*

                                ★

Imagine now at night:

    when the park gates are majestically black and bolted,
        how the stars settle on the sacred ceiba
            and streams of Royal Agave coveting their own hearts;

    how pale florets glisten on the gorgon arms of euphorbias,
        while the Apple Cactuses undress blossom after blossom
            for the celestial moths and bats;

    how the pond mirrors the moonlit sky, while the reed beds shift
        about in the muck, glib as the tortoises,
            the air stilled by their submarine magic.

Here we might chance upon the inhuman – and its modern worship.

Haiku for the Anthropocene

I. *CEIBA INSIGNIS* (WHITE SILK FLOSS TREE)

Ancient sun of gold,
smuggled down this studded trunk
to Earth's underworlds.

2. *CEREUS PERUVIANUS* (PERUVIAN APPLE OR APPLE CACTUS)

> In the deep of night:
> a rush of moons flowering,
> soon rustling with moths.

3. *ECHINOCACTUS GRUSONII* (GOLDEN BARREL CACTUS)

Burrs of lemon spill
themselves, a cascade of fuss
down volcanic rock.

4. *CLEISTOCACTUS WINTERI* (GOLDEN RAT TAIL)

Such obscene sea-green
swarming hardly belongs in
this frankness of sun.

5. *EUPHORBIA CAPUT-MEDUSAE* (MEDUSA'S HEAD)

Its skyward forays
thwarted, it lies low, seething —
bursts with its own stars.

6. *ECHINOPSIS SPACHIANA* (TORCH CACTUS)

> A forest, they rise
> to the god of night and, awed,
> ignite in blossom.

7. *AGAVE FRANZOSINI* (GREY GHOST)

What a soul baring:
all this barbed glory laid out
for the noonday sun.

8. *AGAVE VICTORIAE* (ROYAL AGAVE)

The sky glows with fires.
Grown in the slow kiln of night,
porcelain flowers.

The Bean Seller's Tale

Once upon a time,
we were cast as
hoodwinkers, thieves,
old-timers of the deranged forests
and scarecrow-less fields,
peddling trickery and bedlam
from our ragtag sleeves
to the hungry children
sent far from home.
Yet here you are, all grown,
tendering these gold coins to me
in your open palm.
Well then,
take this unlikely sachet.
Prepare to be humbled all over again.
First, entomb that dust as if
it was the enchanted must
of a dead tyrant
from the faraway
of the nursery room.

And then –
Gogmagog, Blunderbore,
Fee-fi-fo-fum!
You know the routine.
If you feel fear,
run to your mother –
no need for shame.
She has always tended
the secrets of our trade.
Listen to her explain.
Life is a giant,
but it wants nothing
other than to keep on being born.

Scenes from a Documentary

I. URSUS MARITIMUS (POLAR BEAR)

A clash of icebergs   △□◇▷◁◇□▽   strewn on the frozen shore.
        The wind and the wandering animal   ∼   are dreamed
                by the blinding   ∼   drifts of snow.

She haunts the fault lines   ∧ ∼ ∧   where currents fracture pack ice.
    Where gluts of seals   ⅄   gush up
    and slap the cold like mud.

She claws a hole   ○   in the permafrost
        and   ●   entombs   ●   herself.
            Inside the fevered den   ◎   she turns like a trapped compulsive.
        ●

Tends her newborn cub like a wound.

2. *ARACHNOCAMPA LUMINOSA* (GLOW WORM)

Inside this buried space   ⊞   the stars are cannibals.
     The cave   drips   with the secrets
         of their   ●   grave hunger.

So far beneath ground   sky should be   meaningless.
     Yet this black   ■   of dank rock
         gloams   ✧ ¤ ✝ ✧ ¤   with its own infernal galaxy.

A mosquito births   ⇧   onto the surface   ●   of a still pool.
     The glitter of night   provides direction
         with pinpoints of light   [|||]   that drool.

3. *CHELONIA MYDAS* (GREEN SEA TURTLE)

It is an orgy   of waste and emptying   ○   ○   ○
     this spilling of   herself   for hours   into sand.
                Afterwards she melts   ≈   into the sea.

They awaken   from a dream   of yolk and albumen
       into   ∴   suffocating   ∴   graininess.
                Sense the glamour of vastness   ∞   its ease.

Together they   clamour   for the mere chance   of it.
    In reckless flight   they reach this   ⋛   buoyancy
           rich with floating   ξϑϑ϶   wilds of sargassum.

60

4. *APTERYX AUSTRALIS* (SOUTHERN BROWN KIWI)

Come night   𝐂˙ it re-assembles itself   of bewitched sticks.
                like a cluster   ⫶′ˊˋ ˏˊˏ
                      Scuttles mulch   with its   tactless beak.

It finds   a dusty and wingless   ghost   of itself.
        They fuss about   ✓×↓×↘   until they unearth
                 a marriage   ᏮᎧ   of camouflage and blindness.

The egg   ∪ soaks   ∩   in the moon's pallor
         while the birds probe   ⅋   rich thickets   ⅋   of smells
                 that the night   exhumes   for them.

61

Chernobyl Redux

The earth has always been so accommodating,
        enfolding all kinds of calamities: the meteoric end
of dinosaurs, the Neanderthals and other botched experiments,
        the debris of bronze and iron ages, modern battlegrounds ...

And there is still so much space! For us to tuck away
        these bulldozed villages, lorries loaded with fallout,
electrically charged farm animals (appropriately neutralised),
        even a pine forest (gamma-rayed). Pat it all down.

Permit yourself to rest without a bothersome pop or tick.
        (We have reinforced concrete for those more insistent
sounds – the kind that leach the pigment from eyes,
        blister hearts as they beat ...)

2. BIO–ROBOTS

What a piece of work is Man! A wise industrial sentiment –
and too often overlooked in newfangled forecasts of automation.
Lest we forget: that remote-controlled backhoe committed harakiri
from the clifftop of reactor 3, after reaching its emissions capacity …
and look who saved the day! Triumphant as a plague,
crawling out of the rabbit hole of history
in wave after wave, armoured in medieval scraps of lead
and muzzled for respiration. (*Pig-faced*, as the jesters said!)
They had 40 seconds to shovel contaminants (flung from reactor 4)
off the tower's precipice. (We had plans for mass burial down below …)
Have faith, we said, there is nothing *terrifying* up there –
but best to run like the dog, flee like the hare.
Scoop a spadeful or two of that hot stuff away and scram!
Before your bones and teeth are meaningless …
How they moved, like *roof cats!* It was only afterwards they stopped,
slumping together in the sheltered halls like litters of stillborn …
Mind you, some of them are still ticking.
(We had to ban embalming and open caskets …)
100 roubles is all it took – so many bought it.
Of course, we honoured their corps in cement, right at ground zero,
where the birds have returned, against all those glum forecasts.
Listen to them: chirruping away with the Geiger counters.

3. DARK TOURISM

Today we celebrate the half-life of caesium-137
with this sceptical offer: one-day tours only for US$!
Exchange phones for dosimeters and be mesmerised
as battery-powered crickets stridulate in a peace that is
truly ionising. Visitors are most welcome to observe
swans silvering in the cooling pond of radionuclides.
Drip-feed the gargantuan catfish (not recommend for eating).
Glimpse the barn swallow that haunts the excavator
parked outside the sarcophagus, the bird's pale throat
a world first in partial albinism. Marvel at our mushrooms,
21.88 microsieverts' worth and prized by bank voles
with cataracts – so rare! No need to fear our wolves;
they thrive on dogs left over from the original liquidators.
But best to update your shots; even rabies blossoms here!
How fortunate to have liberated Earth of some people.
And thanks to the rich and varied lives of plutonium,
we are guaranteed to be more or less free of human habitation –
and open for business – for another 24,000 years.

4. THE RED FOREST

Dress the wicker basket with cloth and sash.

Set it on the path through the woods.

Perhaps a bear, a boar, a raven, a bee ...

The children have been sent from the village.

All the horses have been shot.

Wind fills the grass with its emptiness.

Once there was a hunter, a dwarf, a witch, a seamstress ...

Who will sew up the tear in the fabric of the world?

5. WHAT WAS INVISIBLE NOW BECOMES VISIBLE

Dew   reconstructs
the   spider's   abstract
longing   for   itself.

The   jaw   of   a   waking   fox
unlocks   the   silence
of   teeth.

Lichen   brushes   the   lips
of   the   stag   burdened
by   dreams   of   lightning.

Potatoes   push   up   from
the   earth   like   nubs
of   bones.

The   moon   is   the   ghost
of   a   rock   in
the   broken   sky   of   dawn.

The   sun   has
already   discovered   everything   including
what   we   have   done.

Fractured States of America

I. SPACE JUNK

God knows, the heavens had delivered all manner of disasters
to the upstanding people of Tulsa, Oklahoma:
deluges, tornadoes. Now what?
Searing the city skyline, after midnight,
this sphere of flame in cherry, sapphire, stunning white.
It reminded Betty of the compact and righteous fury
of the Good Lord, but also (if she was honest)
high-school experiments with Bunsen burners.
Betty was Baptist, but no creationist.
As she watched from her kitchen window,
        she felt there was a lesson in the fireball's silence.

When one blazing light became two, Betty wondered
if she might be witnessing a star birthing.
Skyscrapers blocked her view.
Pragmatic about her health – her body was like a dog that needed
regular walking (regardless of her irregular hours at work) –
she laced her trainers and headed down the hall before she paused,
recalling her grandmother's account of the race massacre of 1921.
The National Guard had bombed Black Wall Street (as it was called)
with homespun turpentine bombs, destroying thirty-five blocks of
businesses and family dwellings, killing hundreds.

        It had not made it into history books at school.

Betty remembered how some of the mysteries of the New Testament
were forbidden. The First Apocalypse of James
had been found in an Egyptian dump, scattered with tax receipts

and bills of sale for donkeys, all scrawled on papyrus.
She locked the door and took to the city outside,
so polluted by artificial light
that respecting the traditional order of day and night
seemed a pointless ritual. She wondered what it meant
for a star to be dividing. Perhaps conquering?
The Creek had named this place Tallasi,

     before it became the Oil Capital of the World.

Betty knew many things, but what she did not know was this:
a Delta II rocket, having thrust
a military satellite into low-Earth orbit, was falling.
The plan: covert reabsorption into atmosphere.
Yet here it was, revelling in the exotic chemistry of heat,
shapeshifting in the lusty throes of transubstantiation –
until it hit a cold snap
and a piece of fuel tank was haphazardly trapped
in an organic shape: a leaf, the colour of ash.
It drifted (naturally) towards a stand of oak trees where

     it glanced off Betty's tracksuited back.

Later, she was told the chances were one in a trillion.
Let the mathematicians fuss over calculations; she knew
that only a miracle had spared her
from the 250-kilogram mutant propellant chamber recovered in Texas.
She had been touched in the dark with such tenderness,
though when she interrogated the object with her fingernail,
it pinged like steel.
She remembered the story of Chicken Licken.
How she longed for the city to wake up.
Come dawn, she took her piece of sky to the municipal library

     for cross-referencing against a history of revelations.

Frank was sleeping in Tampa, Florida, when the land disappeared,
   abducting him and his second-hand bed.

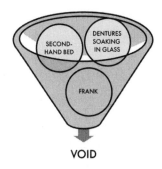

Emergency services quickened to the alien pit
   rimmed with torn ground-slab concrete, ragged fibro

and hairy plaster bits. The hole was deep.
   They lowered in a listening device, but not one word

came from down below. 'A piece of me,'
   Frank's brother told the *Tampa Bay Times*, 'is gone.'

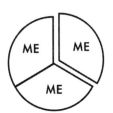

Engineers poured in low-slump aggregate grout,
        a freelancer released a camera drone,

and authorities roped off the scene.
        The insurance company, robbed even of breath by such

collapses of the firmament, had nothing left to give.
        The situation had become so unbalanced.

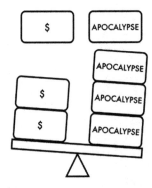

Earth itself was now more of a threat
        than terrorists. It obeyed no code of ethics.

It even stole from the retired, leaving funereal holes
        in their manicured lawns.

In the trailer park, a young mother of six said the disappearing
        reminded her of giving birth, only in reverse.

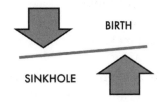

The world is reeling. Who would have thought
Mother Nature could do this to us?

3. ICEBERG WRANGLER

Yes, ma'am, I can tell you that more and more of these mammoths
are calving from Greenland and moseying
down past Newfoundland on the Labrador current,
creating almighty havoc in the North Atlantic shipping lanes.
Who will ever forget the *Titanic*? And the shrimp trawler
BCM Atlantic? She sank in five minutes flat just last year.
My heart may be in Arkansas but I know that God needs me
right here, protecting the good men and women
of the Hibernia platform, drilling for crude in wild ocean,
with storm petrels crashing their lights and flare stacks.
These fine people risk everything
so that we can enjoy the great American life.
My daddy raised me on horseback and 100 acres of black cattle.
Riding on the *Norseman* (a 4,600-ton ship with a steel-reinforced hull),
I take lengths of polypropylene 1,200 feet long – and yahoo!
That rope starts out 8 inches thick and comes back
gnawed as if by a hungry camel.
These free-roaming bergs can be the size of football fields
so if one bucks or kicks ... well, you have to be real careful
and slow. We tow at 1 knot or so.
My daddy always said to remember that I have a greater power
of understanding. And now I know
exactly when these rogues are close to breaking,
because they make a noise – they call it the Bergie Seltzer.
It sounds like a basket of chicken
sinking into an oceanic vat of oil.

Rock

We came to bear witness – via a cinema screen –
to the boat rocking like no cradle we had ever seen.
You were on it; men and women were on it;
children were on it; babies were on it.

(Can I tell you that I have never felt more disgust
at the mindless momentum of the sea,
and where it originated, and why
that movement replicated itself, over and over again?)

There was an immensity of space
above you, tinted a distant blue,
and it was clear that none of us would mean anything
unless we, like gods, decided to.

A handful of people – so small –
stood on the black and jagged rocks
of a shore more hostile than any metaphor.
They watched you lurch and plunge

on those relentless and abominable waves,
before they skittered away from the ocean spray
like mountain goats from a rockfall.
(I apologise; I did nothing to save you.)

Messages from Medellín, the Murder Capital

I can't get through to you, but I have recorded the noise on my phone so that you can hear it when I get home.

It seems to be coming from everywhere and nowhere, as if the papered walls of this hotel room are just a set piece.

As if there is a machine hidden at the heart of the city, producing this grotesque reverberation.

Manufacturing this nightmare of sound.

Come dawn, doves alight on the railing of my balcony, and the darkness and its noise are suddenly gone.

My eyes are raw from tiredness, but the poetry festival starts today.

The press event is in the conference room, and one of the organisers has just begun by reciting the body count of *la violencia*.

A local woman speaks sluggishly of the tortured and the missing, as if she is speaking from somewhere underground, as if she is instructing us in a difficult language.

She was holding a hand over her mouth, keeping in whatever it was that wanted to come out.

There are no trigger warnings.

A Chinese poet shares a dream she had last night.

At least that is what her translator says.

Now a child sings.

If there was such a thing as natural justice, surely we would all be saved.

Afterwards I walk to the Botero Plaza and glimpse a mother and child on a side street, peering into a ragged hole in a bitumen road, cordoned off with strips of decaying plastic.

It seems there is a colossal tunnel made of concrete running beneath the city, hiding a chaos of cables and pipes, all stagnating in a brown bath.

I have just tried to call you from my room, but there is still no signal.

This evening I had my first reading at a town hall.

I read 'Narcissism' – you know – the poem that dismembers bodies into their constituent parts in a game of defamiliarisation.

I hammed it up for laughs.

Now it remains to forgive myself.

I can barely think for fatigue, but what I think is that I made a mistake in coming here.

I have nothing to offer these people.

With words that violate simply for the sake of poetry.

It is privilege, not pain, that makes me articulate.

Endlessly and mindlessly grinding.

The night noise in my hotel room once again is a horror show.

I imagine you and our son lit up by the antipodean day, shining like something quiet and impossible.

Two-and-a-half million people live in this city, its houses sprawling up the mountainside from the valley, as if poverty might defy gravity.

As if humans need not be ground down.

From my balcony I see them, buried by the Andean night.

The darkness is electric with their insomnia.

Murder Mystery

In Memory of WM

1.

I was sitting cheered by the blaze of the TV watching *Midsomer Murders*
when the screen went cockeyed and I was no longer convincing *can you*
see my name? were the last words I pushed through the technology *am I*
still on? was only a thought because there was not enough electricity

2.

Your wife was by the set and she saw what happened at first she thought
the glitch was with your ego but then she called for the repair man of course
it was too late but your children and grandchildren are now saying your lines –
Sweet Jesus, Sod's Law – as if they were plugged in or being directed

Routine Elegy

In Memory of PM

Your mother gets ready for bed, tucking herself in with rigour and method.

With the covers quiet, she sighs into the night, *Well, that's another day gone.*

She is speaking to her husband. He has passed away, but he was always taciturn.

Her voice reaches us through our bedroom wall, as if the plasterboard, come nightfall, turns supernatural.

Our son, an early bird, is tasked with the responsibility of waking her.

She opens her eyes to the dawn and exclaims, *Oh, thank you!* Her enthusiasm frightens him.

She bustles to get ready as though for a birthday party, not even bothering with her hearing aids.

But the gift of the day is snatched away before it can even be opened.

Goldilocks Has Gone Missing

In Memory of GQ

The cottage had been hollowed by the child's death.

Still, Mamma made the porridge, strong-minded as a witch.

The highchair splintered from the weight of so much eeriness.

Then baby was born, filling the void with her fleshiness.

Her eyes were bright, and she felt keenly as infants do.

That was how she discovered the wound, glassy as a window.

It was then she saw the other one.

Vanishing, vanishing, still vanishing

through the crash of it.

Night, Falling
In Memory of CR

What did you see as night was falling?

The vastness of plains, grass furtive with knowledge, and then darkness deepening.

Did the world speak to you as to a shaman?

There are always signs and daemons, but they were no longer for me to speak or sing.

Was it so dark you could not see?

At first there was a moon, shedding its bony light.

Did others hold you?

There were so many – of my own skin and smell and hair and blood – but I alone was being ravaged.

Did you feel the presence of god?

Only love, and the unbearable tragedy of its passing.

Did sleep finally come for you?

The night always comes from within.

And when you woke?

My body was quiet as a beast with its throat cut.

And now?

Can't you feel it? Life is still longing for us, calling for our poetry, our songs.

Teaching My Son Finnish

1.

When I was a child *suomi oli minun kotini*.
The sound of it alone made me safe and whole.

2.

Then *englannin kieli* leveraged a hairline crack …
and soon the whole house was gone.

3.

Hyvää huomenta, I chant to my son each dawn.
Hyvää yötä, I whisper before sending him to sleep.

4.

As if the pagan blessing of sunlight and midnight might help
us both – *kadonneita lapsia* – find our way home.

Night: A Personal History

I.

Night has settled with dew, but there's a fat candle of moon
    so the land is still shapely. Muscular eucalypts and tussock

rise from the paddocks, and the dam distils the blank complexity
    of the galaxy into something like a miracle.

A frog breathes in the reeds near the dank waterline, regurgitating air
    into sound. Even if I went looking, I wouldn't find it.

The night owns everything, including dreams. It has no need for curiosity.
    Earth is cold here, but I can see the stars where the chemicals

now chilling my throat were kilned. When I was born, those elements stunned
    my amniotic lungs and took possession of me, heart and soul.

2.

Tonight, under these headlights, the world bordering the road is sketchy,
as if the landscape has yet to be drawn in.

Marshlands can have that quality; they're imagined as sylvan –
though the truth is we're not paying enough attention.

We're joy-riding, planning to spend eternity in our bodies, as only
teenagers can. If we know anything, out on this ugly smudge of bitumen,

it's that we're all vagrants, uncared-for. The secret of our freedom.
When we hit a ditch, thick with crickets and ti-tree scrub, the car

is junked. The planet moves in its obscure way until dawn discovers us
with hangovers. Then how we shine, like tin cans in the sun.

3.

Another night, and slow eucalypts are creaking. The wind is invisible,
   but doesn't care if we hear it stressing timber

or if we see the canopies, silhouetted by moonlight, violated by its will.
   Down below, the earth, like something brought indoors, is quiet.

There's a dry floor of crushed bark and leaves, the smell of soil and insects,
   air that's museum-still. Lying on our backs we observe

a shroud of stars, vast beyond all knowing, beyond all the groaning
   and swaying. A cigarette is lifted to your lips, then mine.

Our lust was more than rebellion. It was what we held
   against the eternity of night's indifference.

4.

Sometimes night, faceless as a god, communicates to me,
    secretly, the truth of its immensity. It's then I know that terror

is the ur-theory of physics, the dark energy of the cosmos,
    and I'm surprised again by what we can live through.

When the dawn light, birthed in the sun's core 30,000 years ago,
    breaches my bedroom window, it may be a personal blessing

or a celestial war. Either way I rise to its call, while that wind of protons
    and electrons ricochets off Earth's atmosphere and streams, for eons,

through a charnel house of planets and moons and bodies of ice to the end,
    where it's finally shocked by a darkness that is terminal.

5.

I can still feel it tonight, despite my cortical evolution:
    the animal drag, the quiet fury.

Darkness liquesces and which one of us keeps our reason, truly?
    Somewhere in our flesh and blood, we know we were never

meant to survive under this stuff, which shrinks mountains
    into molehills. Grinds ashes to ashes, and dust to dust.

When day breaks, like a bonus, we run polished SUVs over
    our vulnerability, deny the world is round, invent afterlives

somewhere over the rainbow. As if night gave a fuck about our fantasies.
    We invented sedatives for this, but sleep is only fleeting.

6.

There's an existential darkness, as people know – in Van Diemen's Land,
    Dachau, Myanmar – where it's suddenly shown that night

is a euphemism, and the whole universe, considered in its blindness
    and breadth, is vile. That's why our dreams of heaven always

occupy a daytime sky. Gods drift across a blue screen painted for the stage
    with colonnades, a fantasy of marble and lapis lazuli for aristocrats.

Look at the cherubs parading and marauding there, their campness
    an affront to suffering, while the cosmos flows like molasses

and we turn our backs on everything we have ever done.
    One day Earth will rise to kill us. There will be nowhere to go.

Coda

On Happiness

History recognises Turun Söl as a standard disappointment in the ancient practice of poetry (/ˈpəʊɪtri/ *n*. Now rare. Solitary word game played by the melancholy and narcissistic). While Söl's name has become synonymous with an excessive form of morbid verse, it should be noted, if the translations of Söl's soot-stained diaries are to be trusted, that the poet's quest may have originally been optimistic. One must keep in mind that Söl's goal was never to describe mirth or excitement, which are merely temporary conditions, easily tainted by inebriation or *Schadenfreude*. The object of the poet's mission was more stable and pure. Yet evidence of it was so ambiguous. Like pain, it was hard to credit in others. In fact, there was always the possibility that it did not exist at all. One could contrive its appearance simply by being acquiescent and inactive, as a monk or husband might. In any case, it was important to adopt an attitude of scepticism in order not to appear a sentimental fool. The greatest difficulty posed by Söl's subject, of course, was that it avoided words as if they carried the plague. It protected itself like a blue-blood bounded by forest-fed walls of fire. It destroyed images of itself before they could be generated – the ultimate iconoclast, one might say. In the end, Turun Söl is said to have found herself writing obsessively about her subject's manifold and miserable antitheses, such that it seems she herself wondered if language was invented for the sole purpose of expressing pain.

Notes

The epigraph is an excerpt from 'Paris VI, 29, Rue Cassette, Monday, June 24, 1907' from *Letters on Cézanne* by Rainer Maria Rilke, edited by Clara Rilke, translated by Joel Agee. Translation copyright © 1985, 2002 by Farrar, Straus and Giroux. Reprinted by permission of North Point Press, a division of Farrar, Straus and Giroux.

'Nox' takes its title from Anne Carson's elegiac book of the same name.

'Shadow' takes its title from Edgar Allan Poe's 'Shadow: A Parable'. The line 'The red ring of the terrible Saturnus' also comes from that short story.

'Waking in the Blue' takes its title from Robert Lowell's poem of the same name. The phrase 'old-timers' references the use of that phrase in Lowell's poem.

'Lullaby' takes its title from Anne Sexton's poem of the same name. The line 'a goat calls in his dreams' and the phrase 'hush-a-bye' also come from Sexton's poem. These lines are reprinted by permission of SLL/Sterling Lord Literistic, Inc. Copyright by Linda Gray Sexton and Loring Conant, Jr. 1981.

'Argument' takes its title from Elizabeth Bishop's poem of the same name. The word 'gentle' references the use of that term in Bishop's poem.

'Shattered Head' takes its title from Adrienne Rich's poem of the same name. The line 'Revenge on the mouth packed with its inarticulate confessions' also comes from there. Copyright © 2016 by the Adrienne Rich Literary Trust. Copyright © 1999 by Adrienne Rich, from *Collected Poems: 1950–2012* by Adrienne Rich. Used by permission of W. W. Norton & Company, Inc.

'Daddy' takes its title and the line 'you bastard, I'm through' from 'Daddy' in *The Collected Poems*, Sylvia Plath. Copyright © 1960, 1965, 1971, 1981 by the Estate of Sylvia Plath. Used by permission of HarperCollins Publishers. This line is also reproduced with permission from Faber & Faber Ltd.

'Knife' takes its title from Charles Simic's poem of the same name. The phrase 'father-confessor' also comes from there.

'Déjà-vu' makes reference to the German word '*ich*', repeated in Plath's 'Daddy'.

'Liquidation' takes its title from the name – liquidators – given to the men deployed in the immediate aftermath of the 1986 Chernobyl nuclear power plant accident.

The italicised word 'terrifying' in 'Bio-robots' references a speech made by General Nicolai Tarakanov to the reservists assembled beneath the roof of reactor 3, just before they were sent up to clear the radioactive debris that had fallen there: 'Comrades, you should know … that I was up on the roof two days ago with an officer, and one thing for sure I can tell you is that there's nothing terrifying.' Another italicised phrase, 'pig-faced', references the so-called 'pig muzzle' masks worn for protection, while 'roof cats' was another name given to the liquidators.

'Dark Tourism' is named after a type of tourism to places associated with death and suffering. Various companies offer tours of Chernobyl. The maximum length of a visit there is two days.

'The Red Forest' takes its title from a place in the Chernobyl Exclusion Zone so named because the needles of pine trees turned red following exposure to radiation. The trees were subsequently bulldozed and interred. The accident at Chernobyl is said to have contaminated the environment twenty times more than the atomic bombings of Hiroshima and Nagasaki combined.

'What Was Invisible Now Becomes Visible' takes its title from words spoken by the biologist Professor Timothy Mousseau, who has studied the effects of radiation on the flora and fauna of Chernobyl. In 2014 video footage, Professor Mousseau sprays water onto an irregularly shaped spider web and declares, 'What was invisible now becomes visible.' This phrase is reproduced with the kind permission of Timothy Mousseau.

'Fractured States of America' originated in news reports, and the characters imagined in its three poems are based on real people. 'Space Junk' is inspired by the story of Lottie Williams, the first and only person to be hit by space debris, in Oklahoma in 1997. 'Sinkhole Alley' is inspired by the story of Jeffrey Bush, the first man to die in a sinkhole, in Florida in 2013. 'Iceberg Wrangler' relies heavily on the news story 'Iceberg Wrangler', published online in the *Smithsonian Magazine* in February 2003.

'Teaching My Son Finnish' contains a number of Finnish phrases. Their English translations are as follows:

> *suomi oli minun kotini*: Finnish was my home
> *englannin kieli*: the English language
> *hyvää huomenta*: good morning
> *hyvää yötä*: goodnight
> *kadonneita lapsia*: lost children

Acknowledgements

Most of this work was written in Wadawurrung country. I acknowledge the traditional custodians of the land on which I live.

Poems collected here have previously appeared (sometimes in earlier versions) in *The Australian, Australian Book Review, Australian Multilingual Writing Project, Australian Poetry Journal, The Best Australian Poems 2015* (ed. Geoff Page), *2016, 2017, 2018* (ed. Sarah Holland-Batt), *Buying Online: Newcastle Poetry Prize Anthology 2018, Chicago Quarterly Review* (US), *Connotation Press: An Online Artifact* (US), *Cordite Poetry Review, foam:e, Griffith Review, Homings and Departures* (Recent Work Press, 2020), *Inverted Syntax: The Fissured Tongue Series* (US), *Island, Kenyon Review* (US), *Meanjin, #MeToo: Stories from the Australian Movement* (eds Miriam Sved, Christie Nieman, Maggie Scott and Natalie Kon-yu), *Rabbit*, Red Room Poetry's website, *Revista Prometeo* (Colombia), *Signs: The University of Canberra Vice-Chancellor's International Poetry Prize 2018* (eds Jen Webb and Donna Maree Hanson), *Sleazemag, Stilts, Wisconsin Review* (US) and *Writing to the Wire* (eds Dan Disney and Kit Kelen). My thanks to the editors of these journals and anthologies for their support and for providing hard-won opportunities for poetry to be read.

Special thanks to Red Room Poetry's New Shoots project for commissioning 'Guilfoyle's Volcano' for the Royal Botanic Gardens Victoria, where it is 'planted', as well as for commissioning the other botanical and zoological poems in the third section of this book; Andrew Ford for setting part of 'Night: A Personal History' in his extraordinary song cycle *Nature*; Jorge Salavert for his superb Spanish translations of poems for *Revista Prometeo* and for my performances at the 2017 Medellín International Poetry Festival in Colombia; Prithvi Varatharajan and John Kinsella for their professional support and kindness; Gregory Day for suggesting I start thinking about this poetry collection; and Sarah Holland-Batt, Michelle Cahill, Lisa Gorton and Carrie Tiffany for responding so generously to this manuscript.

Heartfelt thanks to Felicity Plunkett for her editorial stewardship of this book, the likes of which I have never experienced in poetry publishing; to Aviva Tuffield for such a warm and wonderful welcome to UQP; and to Felicity Dunning for her invaluable advice and fine-tuning.

My parents' first home in this country was a migrant hostel, but their hard work and belief in the value of education are what enabled me to have a writing life, and I will be eternally grateful to them. My sister, Tiina Takolander, and her daughters, Charlie Burton and Cassidy Quarrel, inspire me with their strength and love and sense of humour. A warm mention to Kate McCooey, Phillis Broadhurst and John McCooey. Thanks to Kate Hall, Jo Langdon and Maria Vella for their encouragement. And thanks to CM, because it was never poetry that saved me.

Finally, thanks to my husband, David McCooey, and our son, Samuel Takolander, for everything, not least of all happiness.